Accent Reduction for

Speakers of Russian

by Ivan Borodin

Copyright 2014

Copyright 2014 by Ivan Borodin

Printed and bound in the United States of America. All rights reserved. No part of this book may be reproduced in any form by electronic or mechanical means, including information storage and retrieval systems, without written permission from Ivan Borodin, except in the case of brief quotations embodied in critical articles and reviews.

ISBN-13: 978-1499739480

ISBN-10: 1499739486

Cover by Pete Sain

Introduction

A thick accent is a colorful gift that no one either wants or deserves. Trying to reduce an accent can feel like a social experiment gone horribly wrong. Words become gasps as they reluctantly rattle from your throat.

When our ideas are lost in the blur of an accent, all parties suffer—especially when the speaker is Russian. The Russian people are courageous and muscular storytellers. They aren't shy about discussing a wide range of topics, from light and funny to dark and tragic. Russians have an ear for the subtleties of the world—both the country they left and the new society in which they dwell. The intelligence, sensibilities and wit of the Russian belong at the table of American conversation.

Let this book serve as a safe initiation into the American accent. Don't wait for perfect conditions. Hit the ground running, becoming comfortable with the various vowel and consonant changes. Don't stop until your head sinks into your pillow at night, your mind swimming with the sounds of your new American voice.

To ease your transition, the bulk of this manual can be found spoken aloud online. Search YouTube for **IvanBorodin** and **Accent Reduction for Speakers of Russian**, then listen to the explanations and drills.

I wish you the very best of good fortune on your journey to speaking English like an American.

1
Syllable Stress

The typical Russian struggles with American English. I have heard it likened to being dropped in the ocean. A Russian once expressed to me that he believed accent reduction was a euphemism for endless torture.

Let this lesson start off with some good news. Going back the last seventy years, with the advent of television, a standard American accent has developed. Some call it media-ese. It is essentially the patterns of pronunciation that the world most quickly identifies as American. These characteristics are reflected in certain vowel and consonant changes.

2

What's the good news? The American accent, for all its complexities, has at least assumed a fixed identity, and is unlikely to change during your lifetime. You should only have to learn this system once.

Understanding the American accent begins with determining which syllable the American emphasizes.

May I take you through a crash course in linguistics? I would be derelict in my duties if I failed to establish a foundation for us to build on.

A **vowel** is a speech sound made by letting breath flow out without closing any part of the mouth or throat. Vowels are represented in English most commonly by the letters A, E, I, O, U and sometimes Y (as in *pretty* and *gym*). The word *vowel* originates from the Latin and French words for voice. The spelling of the two words *voice* and *vowel* remain similar today, which serve as a reminder that vowels are the most basic components of speech.

As a veteran speech instructor, I have learned not to take the student's understanding of vowels and consonants for granted, so how about a brief test? Which of the following are NOT vowels?

1. A C E O I
2. U A M O E
3. I S U E A

Answer Key:	1. C
	2. M
	3. S

A **consonant** is a speech sound made by partly or completely stopping the flow of air through the mouth. Consonants are represented by the letters B, C, D, F, G, H, J, K, L, M, N, P, Q, R, S, T, V, X, Z and sometimes Y (as in *yellow*).

Many speech manuals discuss vowel placement, insinuating that the production of certain vowels occur in different sections of the mouth. However, the production of vowels is of secondary importance to the formation of consonants, which hold a ruler's position in the realm of speech.

Foreign speakers can feel overwhelmed at first by everything they need to consider. Learning the basic terms early will pay dividends when we venture into polishing your pronunciation.

How about a pop-quiz on consonants? Can you find the letter in each list that is NOT a consonant?

4.   B   C   E   F   G
5.   H   I   J   K   L
6.   M   N   O   P   Q

Answer Key:	4. E
	5. I
	6. O

It's time to introduce the most important term of this manual. A **syllable** is a word or part of a word which contains a single vowel sound. It is the smallest division of actual spoken speech. Here are some examples of single syllable words.

so, her, split, wolf, all, bit

In many cases, a word may be written with two vowels, but will only be pronounced as a single syllable, for only one of the vowels are actually pronounced.

feet, great, years, please, soon, sound, lone, blue, tough, side

Many English words contain two syllables. In most cases, either the first or second syllable will be emphasized.

winner, below, beauty, because, ready, again, saving, chatter, silence, arrange, announce

There is no rule that dictates which syllable receives emphasis. Each word must be learned on an individual basis. For this reason, correct syllable stress will generally be underlined throughout this manual. If all the Russian speaker did was emphasize the proper syllable in polysyllabic* words, that action in itself would greatly improve his or her American accent.

* polysyllabic - having more than one syllable.

9

Words with several syllables often have a designated syllable stress.

<u>gen</u>tlemen, <u>ev</u>eryone, i<u>ma</u>gine, com<u>pu</u>ters, ca<u>si</u>no, e<u>xam</u>ple, <u>im</u>migrants, <u>beau</u>tiful, <u>na</u>tional, i<u>den</u>tify, <u>an</u>ything, psy<u>cho</u>logist, <u>ac</u>tually

The foreign speaker initially considers longer words as enemies to clear communication. However, once designated syllable stress is mastered, a longer word is actually easier for the American to understand, as it exists for a longer length of time, so its clarity doesn't hinge on a single vowel.

Longer words frequently contain more than one stressed syllable. Be sure to descend in pitch on each point of emphasis.

*opp*or*tun*ity, *af*ter*noon*, *desp*er*ado**, *In*di*ana*, *ann*iv*er*sary, *mis*under*stood*

* desperado - a reckless, violent criminal

Many students find inspiration in learning syllable stress. I am often questioned by students as to why no one had ever taught them the importance of informed emphasis. All I can say is that your studies have led you to this discovery. Let syllable stress not just be the gateway to improved English pronunciation, but the start of mastery over the American accent.

12

13

Use Syllable Stress to Descend in Pitch

Most foreign speakers attempt to hide their accents by zipping through their sentences. This tactic is strictly defensive and regretably only serves to reduce one's presence.

These introductory chapters serve as the start of a new, practical approach to pronunciation.

If you listen to how Americans stress their words, you'll hear something you didn't notice before. They tend to go down in pitch on stressed syllables. Take in the pattern of the following sentences:

J<u>o</u>seph l<u>if</u>ted the b<u>o</u>ttle of v<u>o</u>dka.

There is a b<u>ed</u>rock bel<u>ie</u>f that g<u>en</u>ius springs from ins<u>a</u>nity.

Notice how the American descends in pitch on stressed syllables. This is particularly easy to affect in words with more than one syllable. It is not an optional undertaking. If you wish to be understood by Americans, you must provide them with the syllable stress they require. Americans may not recognize the science behind this necessity, but will surely respond either positively or negatively to your pronunciation, depending on whether or not you emphasize the proper syllable in polysyllabic words.

15

I have spent my career helping students recognize the pattern that Americans use to communicate. The students who choose to embrace the use of proper syllable stress report an increased level of clarity and better communication with Americans.

With longer words, the course of action is clear. Identify the stressed syllable—or syllables—then descend in pitch on each of them. But how should a word with only a single syllable be approached?

Let us examine the case of **sentences that lack long words**:

Once the game is done, the king and the pawn go back in the same box.

Syllable stress within such a sentence falls under the category of word stress. The drawback to such a sentence is that it lacks guidelines. However, the upside is that the stress is flexible. Below is an example of how it could be stressed.

<u>Once</u> the <u>game</u> is <u>done</u>, the <u>king</u> and the <u>pawn</u> go <u>back</u> in the <u>same</u> <u>box</u>.

An American might stress the sentence differently to make a specific point (In the following case, the speaker is dramatizing the finality of the consequences.)

<u>Once</u> the game is <u>done</u>, the king and the pawn go <u>back</u> in the same box.

In the following variation, the speaker is drawing a parallel between two opposing stations in class.

<u>Once</u> the game is done, the king <u>and</u> the pawn go back in the <u>same</u> box.

In conclusion: apply word stress—early and often—to single-syllable words. The tendency to descend in pitch on stressed syllables (and single-syllable words) is the connective tissue of the American accent.

Follow suit and use syllable and word stress to create the American rhythm, also known as the American accent.

Understanding the Schwa

ə

a schwa

At this point of the program, a term will be introduced that you won't hear in everyday conversation—the schwa. In a sense, the schwa is the only technical term of this manual. You'll never hear an ordinary American use the word *schwa*, because the typical American already employs it on a regular basis as a matter of course.

While the schwa may come across as a bit scientific, it is absolutely necessary for the development of clear American speech. The schwa is so helpful that nearly every speech instructor employs it. The schwa is a clever, brilliant device, and should become one of your tools in generating an American accent.

Russian speakers often 'over-pronounce' words, meaning they place unnecessary emphasis on unstressed syllables.

The 'schwa' is the universally accepted symbol for a vowel that will not be pronounced as it appears, but rather as 'uh'. Almost every English dictionary uses this symbol, which resembles an upside-down, lowercase E. The schwa also signals to the speaker that the syllable is unstressed.

In the word 'at', the 'a' is pronounced with a short A, as in 'cat'. However, in the word 'announce', the 'a' in the first syllable is a schwa.

21

  ə   ə   ə   ə
announce   unfamiliar   Hawaiian

                            ə   ə
We wish we could once again read the manual.

   ə   ə   ə
Actually, that Honda sells for about twenty grand.

  ə   ə ə   ə   ə
Santa Monica accepted Irena's application for asylum.

  ə   ə   ə   ə
Natasha was disappointed with Sasha.

In the word 'dead', the 'e' is pronounced with a short E, as in 'sent'. However, in the word 'decay', the 'e' in the first syllable is a schwa, and is not fully pronounced.

  ə   ə   ə   ə
de<u>cay</u> *   <u>bu</u>siness   <u>know</u>ledge <u>op</u>en

* the slow destruction of something, possibly from natural events or lack of care.

           ə   ə   ə   ə
It is <u>pos</u>sible he'll be ar<u>res</u>ted by <u>fed</u>eral <u>ag</u>ents.

    ə   ə
I <u>scol</u>ded her for <u>be</u>ing dis<u>hon</u>est.

             ə   ə   ə
You're the <u>per</u>fect <u>per</u>son for your <u>tar</u>get <u>mar</u>ket.

         ə ə ə ə ə   ə
He con<u>sis</u>tently re<u>min</u>ded <u>peo</u>ple to re<u>main</u> <u>con</u>fident.

In the word 'go', the 'o' is pronounced with a long O, as in 'most'. But in the word 'person', the 'o' is reduced to a schwa and is barely articulated.

   ə   ə   ə
p<u>er</u>son   pr<u>o</u>posal   dev<u>e</u>lop

       ə   ə ə
I was con<u>cerned</u> about the coll<u>ect</u>ion material.

        ə   ə
The pr<u>o</u>posal was fouled up be<u>yond</u> all <u>reas</u>on.

      ə   ə   ə ə
The <u>less</u>on is to con<u>struct</u> a <u>work</u>ing sol<u>ut</u>ion.

  ə   ə
<u>Rec</u>ognize the need for new <u>cust</u>omers.

    ə   ə ə
I cong<u>rat</u>ulated him on the suc<u>cess</u>ful <u>dem</u>on<u>stra</u>tion.

Sometimes a pair of vowels become a schwa. In the word 'action', the 'ion' is pronounced as a schwa.

ə
ac<u>ti</u>on

In fact, most -ion endings are pronounced as schwas.

ə   ə   ə   ə   ə
<u>u</u>nion lo<u>ca</u>tion op<u>era</u>tion <u>na</u>tion <u>op</u>tion

By the way, here's a quick tip on syllable stress: In words with -ion endings, the stress often falls directly before the 'ion'.

ə   ə   ə
re<u>ac</u>tion ins<u>pec</u>tion <u>sta</u>tionary

Many common word endings are reduced to schwas.

ə	ə	ə	ə
cer<u>tain</u>	ap<u>p</u>le	an<u>ge</u>l	<u>wo</u>men

ə	ə	ə	ə
<u>for</u>tune	<u>peop</u>le	<u>gar</u><u>b</u>age	<u>priv</u>ate

But not all unstressed endings are schwas:

Ā	Ī	Ō
tee<u>nage</u>	<u>ey</u>esight	<u>bathr</u>obe

'Y' endings are unstressed, though not reduced:

Ē	Ē	Ē	Ē
<u>many</u>	<u>hairy</u>	<u>love</u>ly	<u>def</u>initely

Throughout this manual, the schwa will be marked over select words. This ə symbol indicates that the speaker should reduce the vowel to 'uh', all the while taking care to avoid stressing it, as the schwa is by definition an *unstressed* reduced vowel.

People decide to study accent reduction for many different reasons, one of them being to fit in. Over-pronounced words draw negative attention to the speaker. Becoming aware of which syllables require *less* effort is a key factor in beginning to sound American.

The author acknowledges the challenge the Russian speaker faces upon encountering this awkward symbol. No one appreciates being surprised by—and burdened with—a strange notation.

However, the benefits of mastering this element far outweigh the initial confusion. If the student is willing to try something new—in this case the schwa—their focus will be rewarded with a speech pattern more accessible and familiar to the American ear.

28

29

The Long A

Avoid adding an intrusive 'uh' sound before this pure vowel, as that lends it a British air. Russian speakers also need to differentiate the long A from the short E (as in *get*). This is accomplished by having this long A descend in pitch when it occurs within stressed syllables.

    ə   ə   ə ə   ə ə

p<u>a</u>tient, p<u>ai</u>nter, <u>a</u>ncient, d<u>a</u>ted, deter<u>mi</u>n<u>a</u>tion, game, table, be<u>ha</u>vior, docu<u>men</u>t<u>a</u>tion, del<u>ayed</u>, r<u>ai</u>ning, cont<u>ai</u>ners

                                  ə

What *gave* you the <u>i</u>*dea* that <u>e</u>veryone was *ok<u>ay</u>*?

                   ə

What *makes* the *pop*<u>*u*</u>*l<u>a</u>tion* so sure?

30

Ray thought we were go_ing to *take* turns.

ə

I've had to *train* as hard as <u>ev</u>eryone else to get to this *place*.

I *say* em<u>brace</u> the weird *capes*.

ə

If she is <u>able</u> to *maintain* a <u>stable</u> re<u>lat</u>ionship, she will find *ways* to prove it.

ə

We are each in <u>danger</u> of <u>being</u> con<u>sumed</u> by what we do and how we are.

ə

A *display* of one's work is a <u>naked</u> <u>hist</u>ory of the <u>struggle</u> to re<u>ceive</u> an <u>education</u>.

ə

This is the last <u>generation</u> of *chain* smokers.

You'll <u>nev</u>er look at the *major* leagues the *same way*.

      ə

Are *they* e<u>nough</u> for your first *day* at the new job?

       ə

The *e<u>state</u> <u>ag</u>ents* said *they'd* come to view the *cave*.

  ə   ə   ə ə   ə

I ac<u>know</u>ledge my *li<u>mita</u>tions* and am *<u>grate</u>ful* for <u>ev</u>ery new *day*.

The long vowels covered in this section of the manual could be considered the 'basic' vowels. Mastery over these basics equates to building a foundation for clear American speech.

33

The Long O

Russian speakers have two things to look out for when pronouncing the long O. First off, they must seek to avoid sounding British. If they add an 'ehh' before the O, the vowel will have an English twist. Secondly, Russian speakers should be careful not to turn the long O into AW, effectively flattening the vowel.

    ə   ə

social, golden, yolks, mostly, snowstorm, slowed, so, notepads, closed, ghosts, motion, growing

I don't understand the word 'no'.

You told me they had videos.

34

Get to *know* the nurses' names and they'll *throw* you an e<u>x</u>tra <u>pa</u>tient now and then.

                         ə   ə   ə

Just *don't* make me ap<u>o</u>l<u>o</u>gize for <u>bei</u>ng s<u>ome</u>one <u>peo</u>ple like.

              ə

What are your *goals* for to<u>day</u>?

Let your *hopes*, not your hurts, *mold* your f<u>u</u>ture.

        ə   ə   ə ə

Most <u>sales</u>people have a <u>fa</u>vorite *m<u>o</u>bile* device.

       ə   ə

The <u>num</u>bers <u>were</u>n't <u>clear</u>ly *<u>pos</u>ted*.

      ə   ə

The words were <u>pain</u>ted in a neat, *<u>old</u>-fashioned* arch upon the <u>win</u>dow of the shop.

35

                ə   ə

The <u>*pony*</u>tailed <u>*host*</u>ess in a black <u>T</u>-shirt *ap<u>proach</u>ed* me.

      ə

<u>Ev</u>erybody looked hung <u>*ov*</u>*er* or as if they had just *rolled* out of bed.

                     ə   ə

Be<u>cause</u> <u>noth</u>ing was <u>*op*</u>*en,* I felt a bit lost and <u>didn</u>'t *know* where else to *go*.

To kill some time I walked <u>*ov*</u>*er* to the *old* <u>build</u>ing.

While making your way through this manual, be sure to descend in pitch on stressed syllables, lay off the reduced vowels (marked ə, which means they are pronounced 'uh'), and aim to pronounce the italicized words exactly like an American.

37

The Long E

Russian speakers have two considerations when forming the long E. To avoid sounding British, Russians need to refrain from adding an intrusive 'uh' before the vowel. Russians should also keep in mind that the long E is a sharp, brilliant vowel, and not pronounce it as a short I (as in *win*).

　　　ə　　　　　　　　　　　　　ə
com*ple*te, cheeks, be, weep, streets, <u>nee</u>ded, mean, *e*mail, fees, <u>lea</u>dership, key, sweet, team,

Who do you be<u>lie</u>ve?

　　　　　　ə　　ə　　　　　　ə
All things <u>be</u>ing <u>e</u>qual, <u>would</u>n't you <u>ra</u>ther <u>re</u>pre<u>sent</u> the <u>in</u>nocent?

           ə   ə

It gives *me* the a<u>bil</u>ity to *reach* out and com<u>mu</u>nicate with my <u>au</u>dience with<u>out</u> them *needing* to <u>vi</u>sit my <u>web</u>site.

<u>Ire</u>ne felt sick <u>af</u>ter *she* put down the phone.

<u>Peter</u> <u>realized</u> that *<u>Easter</u>* was a few *weeks* a<u>way</u>.

                  ə   ə

I saw <u>some</u>thing I <u>had</u>n't *seen* before.

<u>Theo</u> took a *deep* breath for <u>courage</u>.

He was at *least* six foot *three*.

                   ə

I would <u>nev</u>er *dream* of sug<u>gest</u>ing such a thing.

          ə   ə

The *green* fe<u>do</u>ra was the type of hat a *leading* man might wear in a <u>mov</u>ie.

39

ə

His hair was <u>mos</u>tly gray and *needed* <u>cu</u>tting.

The <u>num</u>ber of *deals* that pan out is *ex<u>tremely</u>* small.

The *an<u>tique</u> reeked* of oil paint.

His *heels* stuck out of his <u>slip</u>pered *feet*.

The air was <u>al</u>most too stale to *breathe*.

The student should seek to establish a working relationship with these long vowels. Try to get each italicized sound in a given chapter to match the others (i.e. in this case, the vowels *heels* and *feet* should sound the same.)

41

The Long U

There are two pitfalls to avoid when pronouncing the long U.

The first is that Americans tend to have fewer 'Y's before their long 'U's. You will catch the occasional 'y' before a long U, as in *cute* and *accuse,* but British speakers add that 'y' before many words with the long U that Americans pronounce without that 'y', such as *new* and *Tuesday.* Russian speakers need to familiarize themselves with how Americans handle each long U on a case-by-case basis.

The second mistake that a Russian speaker needs to avoid is pronouncing the long U as one of its softer variations, such as mutating the name 'Luke' to 'look'.

42

        ə

new, <u>ru</u>mors, due, who, <u>fu</u>neral, school, room, move

      ə

It's not that *cru<u>ci</u>al*.

     ə   ə   ə

The ca<u>reer</u> crisis <u>tigh</u>tened like a *noose* ar<u>ound</u> my neck.

                          ə

I'll go get my *<u>News</u>week* back from *<u>Ju</u>lian* and see *whose* ca<u>reer</u> is more pa<u>the</u>tic.

It <u>wouldn</u>'t have to *do* with <u>any</u>thing else, would it?

I've been <u>wai</u>ting a week for *you* to tell me.

     ə

We <u>haven</u>'t done <u>low</u>er leg work for *two* weeks.

Who is it?

Why don't we talk about *you* in<u>stead</u>?

43

　　　　ə　　ə
I love p<u>i</u>zza, ba<u>s</u>ketball, old black and white *mo<u>v</u>ies*, and <u>wo</u>men in bi<u>ki</u>nis.

Ex<u>cuse</u> me?

I don't have to *do* this.

I *use* my bare feet to find my way in the dark.

　　　　　　　　　ə　　　　ə　　ə
I was o<u>ver</u>whelmed by the *ac<u>cu</u>mulated* lo<u>ss</u>es.

　　　　ə　　ə　　　　ə ə
Her <u>so</u>lo *de<u>but</u>* an<u>nounc</u>es a re<u>mark</u>able voice.

　　　　ə　　ə
The pa<u>ra</u>normal *in<u>cludes</u>* <u>vam</u>pires, <u>were</u>wolves and <u>any</u>thing that goes bump in the night.

<u>An</u>dy *<u>Roo</u>ney* said that love, not time, heals all *wounds*.

Oppor<u>tu</u>nity is missed by most <u>peo</u>ple be<u>cause</u> it is dressed in <u>o</u>veralls and looks like work.

45

The Final Z

Blame it on the spelling. When the letter S appears at the ends of words, it is often pronounced as a Z. Russian speakers announce their nationality by respecting the written S.

Unfortunately, there are also times when the letter S actually remains an S (as in *else*), and the letter C occasionally behaves like an S (as in *face*). Use the following list as a starting off point to discover where a Z is needed.

46

      ə   ə

as, <u>clo</u>sing, re<u>solved</u>, <u>va</u>lentines, <u>plea</u>sures, <u>lov</u>ers, strings, <u>flow</u>ers

Please, let's have a quick chat.

         ə

Do <u>ei</u>ther of you re<u>mem</u>ber your *dreams*?

How <u>many</u> *times* are they <u>go</u>ing to replay that thing?

So who are we <u>choosing</u>?

       ə   ə   ə

These *kids* have <u>incon</u><u>sist</u>ent defenses.

   ə

In <u>human</u> *<u>mat</u>ters* she <u>nev</u>er for<u>got</u> <u>any</u>thing.

    ə ə   ə

<u>Chal</u>lenges are <u>oppor<u>tun</u>ities</u> for growth.

47

        ə   ə
My *family's* definition of love was Stalin-esque.

                                      ə
The *shades* were down, so it took my *eyes* a moment to adjust.

  ə
Hundreds of get-well *cards* were strung up on ribbons.

               ə ə
The *balloons* hovered ominously at the ceiling.

You *guys* are fine.

49

The Final D

Russian speakers reduce the final D to an aspirated T. This both confuses the American ear and robs the Russian of vibration that comes with a final voiced consonant (which is a hallmark of American tonality).

world, mind, <u>overwhelmed</u>, <u>bed</u>side, lied, <u>Band</u>-Aid, won<u>der</u>, co<u>ve</u>red, swelled, in<u>tend</u>, be<u>hind</u>, fade

You *told* me to watch the *<u>vi</u>deo*.

      ə   ə

<u>Some</u>body *<u>roun</u>ded* up a bunch of <u>bi</u>kers and gave them leg warmers.

      ə

It's the *<u>mid</u>dle* of the day.

      ə

Don't get <u>peo</u>ple *in<u>vol</u>ved*.

50

A trash-can *lid* makes a te<u>rr</u>ific *shield*.

The dog *raised* his *head* and *glared*.

      ə   ə

I had de<u>ve</u>loped the *ten<u>d</u>ency* to get *tired* <u>du</u>ring the day.

                              ə

It was <u>very</u> strange to be *<u>hold</u>ing* <u>some</u>body's *hand*.

          ə

The *<u>slen</u>der <u>hus</u>band had* not <u>under<u>stood</u></u> and *had re<u>fus</u>ed*.

She *seemed* to cope well with the *de<u>mands</u>* of the <u>chil</u>dren.

                                    ə

He *loved* to watch the <u>sun</u>set from the <u>kitch</u>en <u>win</u>d<u>ow</u>.

51

       ə   ə   ə ə   ə ə   ə
She *decided* she *needed* e*mo*tional and fi*nan*cial in*de*pen*dence*.

           ə   ə
He *tried* a *lit*tle *ten*derness.

Chad en*joyed* the *sand*wich you *made* for him.

     ə   ə   ə
She re*garded* the *band* as *won*derful.

                   ə   ə
I saw from his *grizzled* face and cata*ract-clouded* eyes that he was *ve*ry old. *

* cataract - a medical condition that causes the lens in the eye to become white.

53

The Short O

There was a time when Russians learned to speak English solely from teachers who were born in Great Britain. This created a tradition of speaking English with a Standard British accent. That may be perfectly fine if a Russian decides to live in England, but the American ear will only be doubly-confused by a hybrid Russian/British accent.

The European pronunciation of *follow* would be *fawllow,* *wash* would sound like *wawsh, popular* would be *pawpular*. Avoid that by correcting the short O, as in *not*, and pronouncing it AH.

54

  ə   ə   ə   ə ə

ap<u>ol</u>ogy, on, <u>ob</u>viously, <u>co</u>lleagues, pos<u>si</u><u>bil</u>ity, <u>op</u>por<u>tu</u>nity, socks, <u>ob</u>ser<u>va</u>tion, <u>prob</u>ably, be<u>yond</u>, res<u>olv</u>ed

                   ə

Meet me at our <u>u</u>sual *spot*.

                        ə   ə

That *<u>mon</u>ster <u>can</u>not* be al<u>lowed</u> <u>ac</u>cess to my <u>se</u>crets.

           ə   ə   ə ə

The <u>man</u>tle of *res<u>pon</u>si<u>bil</u>ity* weighs on those who choose to ac<u>cept</u> it.

                 ə   ə

The *<u>mod</u>ern* world <u>chang</u>es <u>quick</u>ly and quite <u>of</u>ten.

                 ə

<u>Rog</u>er thought back <u>ov</u>er the *<u>con</u>ver<u>sa</u>tion*.

55

          ə   ə

Your <u>*father*</u> didn't <u>*bother*</u> to ask if there's a <u>*problem*</u> with <u>*pomegranates*</u>.

                                    ə

The <u>*doctor*</u> needs to see how your <u>*body responds*</u>.

              ə   ə ə   ə ə

For a boy in A<u>mer</u>ica, <u>base</u>ball is *not optional*.

         ə   ə ə   ə

The <u>*cottage*</u> was <u>*sui*</u>table for a <u>*prosperous*</u> family.

                      ə

A <u>*comic*</u> book is a <u>*solid object*</u>.

 ə   ə

<u>*Cic*</u>adas* screamed as the sun *dropped* be<u>hind</u> the <u>for</u>est.

* an insect native to hot climates, with large wings, that makes a singing noise.

OO as in 'Look'

The Russian speaker often makes the mistake of turning this short vowel into a long vowel. For example, *look* has a way of becoming *Luke*.

Make a point of learning the American pronunciation of this short vowel.

shook, good, push, pull, <u>*cookbook*</u>

There was a strong smell of *wood* smoke.

He *took* her hand and *stood* be<u>side</u> her. [ə above "side"]

58

      ə

It *shouldn't* be too much of a <u>bo</u>ther.

She *would* be <u>bu</u>sy for the rest of the <u>sum</u>mer.

I don't want to *put* you on the spot.
    ə   ə

The at<u>ten</u>dant said they *would* do the best they *could*.

    ə   ə ə

He *couldn't loo*k at his re<u>flec</u>tion in the <u>mir</u>ror.

  ə

I <u>ma</u>naged to <u>nur</u>ture the hope that he'd *pull* through.

      ə

She *would* have <u>hat</u>ed that.

He *shook* his head as if to clear it.

She's not out of the *woods* yet.

59

      ə

I *pushed* open the door and *stood* <u>look</u>ing <u>in</u>to the <u>dark</u>ness.

She's in a *good* deal of pain.

    ə

I <u>could</u>n't quite get out the words.

     ə

He <u>ma</u>naged to *cook* with one hand and smoke with the <u>o</u>ther.

  ə   ə

A <u>peb</u>ble at that speed is as *good* as a <u>bullet</u>.

             ə

My mouth was so *full* that I <u>could</u>n't talk.

The Unstressed Long E

Russian speakers often learn English through British teachers and examples. While this helps in learning proper grammar, it also contributes to making the Russian sound British. When speaking American English, the Russian needs to adapt to the local custom.

British speakers tend to reduce the unstressed long E to a short I. The ending of the word *study* winds up sounding like *stud-i* as in the word *in*. Americans finish the sound with a long E, as in *key*.

It is somewhat unfair to ask the Russian to tune a vowel that occurs on an unstressed syllable, yet that is exactly what is being asked. Keep in mind that proper syllable stress is the primary concern. Never sacrifice correct stress in pursuit of a vowel correction.

  ə ə   ə   ə
com__pa__nies, as__sem__bly, elec__tri__city, lux__ury, __pre__viously, __new__ly, has__ti__ly, men__ta__lity, __shor__tly, __ful__ly, __cur__rency, com__plete__ly, __har__dly, __di__ligently, __firm__ly

    ə ə ə
He was *__per__sonally* a*__gainst__* the *di__rec__tory* from the *__ve__ry* start.

We watched the *__fac__tory* worker *__quick__ly* and *__ar__rogantly* re*__turn__* all *__i__*tems of *__va__*lue.

  ə   ə   ə
We re*__ceived__* per*__mis__*sion from the *__mi__litary au__tho__rities*.

Ini__tially these con__tacts were *ex__clusively* se__cret in na__ture.

I was far from be__ing sure that the *mon__ey* was *suc__cessfully* del__ivered.

She wore a *daisy* tucked be__hind her ear.

Some__body from the *uni__ver__sity* walked out of the *movie*.

The ac__tors *em__bodied* a cla__ssic wor__king class cou__ple, their cour__tship *re__markably* in__nocent in an out__law world.

Handling the Letter T

The American accent is composed of a few ridiculously inventive quirks, one of them being the glottal stop.

Let us first turn the conversation toward how Americans pronounce the letter T when it appears at the end of a syllable.

Here are four cases, each handled in a slightly different fashion:

$$ə$$
sent, late, party, <u>beauti</u>ful

66

When preceded by either an N or L, the letter T has a greater chance of being articulated. The return of a pronounced T may occur because N and L are both made by the tongue-tip striking the gum ridge behind the upper teeth.

    ə   ə   ə   ə ə
dis<u>t</u>ant, adult, <u>treat</u>ment, i<u>dent</u>ified, <u>diff</u>icult, paint,
tilt, melt, <u>par</u>ent, point, joint, sent, mint

  ə   ə   ə   ə   ə
I *re<u>sent</u>ed* the ad<u>vice</u> of my *op<u>pon</u>ent.*

                       ə   ə   ə
She spoke in her *<u>gentl</u>est,* most hyp<u>not</u>ic voice.

She had a *gi<u>gant</u>ic* fa<u>mi</u>ly.

I *felt* strange <u>ev</u>ery time I *<u>en</u>tered* the mall.

67

    ə   ə   ə   ə

Pre<u>ten</u>ding that *pre<u>s</u>ent* <u>cir</u>cumstances are what you *want* is a form of *<u>fan</u>tasy*.

Why *can't* she stay here?

                            ə ə

He *went* to the *front* of the *<u>e</u>legant* house.

  ə   ə   ə ə   ə ə

I *<u>did</u>n't want* to ex<u>plain</u> the *<u>re</u>cent de<u>ve</u>lopment*.

           ə   ə

All hope <u>va</u>nished the *<u>mo</u>ment* I <u>under</u>stood what he *meant*.

        ə   ə   ə

The *<u>stu</u>dent* was *<u>gran</u>ted* per<u>miss</u>ion to stand in *front* of the *a<u>part</u>ment*.

            ə   ə ə

His dream *as<u>sign</u>ment* was to work on *inde<u>pen</u>dent* films.

It would have *meant* a lot to my fa<u>th</u>er.

             ə ə   ə   ə

The *<u>pro</u>mi<u>n</u>ent* <u>coup</u>les were from *<u>dif</u>ferent* <u>coun</u>tries.

            ə

I was too *im<u>pa</u>tient* to wait.

Americans generally **abstain from pronouncing the final T.** This is because the air will usually be stopped in the vocal folds before the tip of the tongue has a chance to strike behind the upper teeth. In American English, most final T's go unarticulated.

might, white, light, got, cut, tight, out, spot, but

You *ought* to *get* a job.

They re<u>turned</u> home *that night* to *eat* the <u>overcooked</u> meat.

I can't *wait* all *night*.

The man at the *yacht* club *treats* us like old friends.

I *thought* you were watching your *weight*.

She grew <u>*distraught*</u>, *yet* looked *straight at* me. *

* distraught - upset by doubt or mental conflict.

If the letter T appears at the end of a syllable—and between two vowel sounds—it can sound more like the letter D than anything else.

     ə   ə

<u>pret</u>ty, com<u>pli</u>cated, <u>naugh</u>ty, <u>nat</u>ive, <u>figh</u>ting, <u>gla</u>diator, res<u>pon</u>si<u>bil</u>ity, a<u>bil</u>ity

<u>Ken</u>ny found out we were <u>dat</u>ing.

     ə   ə   ə ə
I liked him be<u>cause</u> he <u>treat</u>ed me as a com<u>pan</u>ion.

  ə ə
He <u>vis</u>ited her <u>af</u>ter school.

He was <u>hap</u>py to stand for hours ex<u>plain</u>ing <u>ev</u>ery sin<u>g</u>le <u>it</u>em in the <u>cab</u>inet.

What are you <u>do</u>ing with that <u>wat</u>er?

  ə   ə

He be<u>lieved</u> a <u>mon</u>ster *<u>waited</u>* for him.

            ə

I felt *better* <u>know</u>ing he was <u>on</u>ly a bus ride a<u>way</u>.

One af<u>ternoon</u>, we were *<u>eating</u>* a <u>cher</u>ry tart he'd bought at the <u>farm</u>er's market.

I was a<u>fraid</u> of *<u>getting</u>* in too deep.

      ə   ə

You might have *<u>noticed</u>* how *<u>lit</u>tle* time was spent on *cre<u>ating</u>* art.

ə   ə ə

I en<u>joyed</u> the *<u>beautiful</u> <u>letter</u>* to the *<u>editor</u>*.

        ə ə   ə ə

My <u>smart</u>phone has *un<u>limited</u>* <u>text</u>ing *cap<u>abilities</u>*.

       ə   ə ə ə ə

<u>Many</u> *<u>writers</u>* have <u>point</u>ed out the *<u>positive</u>* <u>ben</u>efits.

           ə ə   ə   ə ə

He spent four *undefeated* seasons in the arena.

       ə ə   ə   ə ə

The *elected representative* proved himself a *traitor*.

      ə ə ə   ə   ə   ə

Los Angeles *Community* College *updated* its website.

The most ignored factor in high-*intensity* bodybuilding is the necessary amount of rest.

The entire issue might be made clear if we looked at it in terms of the body's *capacity* to cope with stress.

          ə ə   ə

Those resources *contributed* to more growth.

    ə   ə

I was aware of music *emanating** from the rear of the apartment.

* emanate - to come from a source: originate

When things get complicated around T-endings, the result—and the centerpiece of this lesson—is **the glottal stop**. In this case, the vocal folds tighten for a brief moment, robbing the tongue of its ability to articulate the T. This complete stoppage of air can be triggered by the stressed syllable ending in a vowel combination (as in *apartment*), or the syllable following the T-ending centering around a consonant such as the letter N (as in *button*). It sometimes just happens because a lax D isn't enough to convey the word (as in *city*).

The technical definition of a glottal stop is the rapid closing of the vocal cords. This occurs even where no

'T' is present, such as the space between the words 'walk back'. What's being analyzed here are the cases where that break between syllables seem to take more than a mere articulated T or D-substitution.

   ə   ə   ə
*ti*tle, *bo*ttles, as*sort*ment, *butt*er

The *shoo*ters were *ea*ting outside.

         ə ə
Which *ci*ty is the *ca*pital?

       ə   ə ə
He had *cer*tainly been con*ver*ted.

           ə ə
She scanned the *bul*letin board.

  ə
He *snor*ted with *laugh*ter.

      ə
Try not to get *bea*ten up on *Satur*day night.

        ə   ə   ə
They seemed not to *no*tice Sasha's entrance.

75

AW needs to sound less British

The American accent is pronounced in the jaw and throat, using less of the facial muscles than British speakers. This difference grows quickly apparent when a Russian speaker pronounces the *aw* sound, which appears in words such as *wall, cost* and *broad*. This sound is correctly produced by lowering the soft palate and focusing the energy of the stressed syllable into the jaw and lower lip.

ə

soft, fall, saw, small, call, <u>wa</u>ter, <u>co</u>ffee, al<u>ong</u>

You were an <u>*awfully*</u> good guest, *Paul*.

I've <u>ne</u>ver been out of the <u>ci</u>ty for <u>*longer*</u> than eight days.

76

ə

It still shocked me, no matter how *often* I *saw* them kissing.

ə

The pill wasn't *strong* enough to knock me out.

ə

The airport was like a *mall*-sized version of Red Square.

It took a *long* time for my bag to come *off* the carousel.

ə

I *fought* to stay awake.

Always carry your portfolio with you when at a convention.

ə

We're not trying to be *all* things to *all* people.

77

         ə

The *author's* passion inspired his book.

      ə

Most women wince at his housekeeping and don't stay *long*.

        ə

I *thought Claudia* was *talking* to me.

    ə   ə   ə

The strangeness exhilarated * me, and *also* frightened me a little.

* exhilarated - feeling happy and excited

79

The Jerk

There is a category of R-endings that sound exactly the same, yet are written with an astonishing variety of letters. For this reason, this irregular R-ending has earned an obnoxious nickname—the Jerk. Consider the following words, and take in the fact that Americans pronounce them all *er*.

turn, perfect, birth, word, earned

Russians tend to open up this R-ending to sound like *air*, which confuses the American ear. The key to mastering this irregularity is to pinpoint one of these words that the speaker already pronounces correctly, and then have the speaker learn to match the other 'jerk'-sounds to the one that is already correctly pronounced.

The *girls* showed up *overdressed*.

I have no *words*.

My heart has been <u>*hurting*</u> <u>*over*</u> it.

          ə
He asked the <u>*visitor*</u> to grab a *shirt*.

               ə
It was the most <u>stress</u>ful thing in the *world*.

        ə   ə
Bale and <u>A</u>dams *worked* with <u>Russell</u> on "The <u>*Fighter*</u>".

I watched that <u>mov</u>ie late-night on my <u>*birthday*</u>.

                                                                ə

He *turned* on the ra<u>d</u>io and pushed the scan <u>but</u>ton.

    ə   ə

What<u>ev</u>er you're <u>hav</u>ing will be *<u>per</u>fect*.

Notice how the spelling of the following words is inconsistent, yet all are pronounced with the same *er* sound.

girls, words, <u>hurt</u>ing, <u>per</u>fect, earned

Americans pronounce these 'Jerk' endings the exact same way—as should the Russian when speaking American English.

Mastering the 'Jerk' is important, because the Russian generally mispronounces it to such a degree that the American is left struggling to divine a word's meaning.

So it's not *airnd,* but *earned*

    not *pairple, but <u>pur</u>ple*

    not *vairb,* but *verb*

                              ə   ə
The film *earned* <u>rough</u>ly three <u>hun</u>dred <u>mill</u>ion.

  ə   ə ə
<u>Pur</u>ple is the best *al<u>ter</u>native* <u>col</u>or.

             ə   ə   ə   ə
The *verb* was <u>op</u>en to *in<u>ter</u>pre<u>ta</u>tion*.

The Short A

Russians have a way with words, and a rather creative method of running vowels across the roof of the mouth. This works fine in Russian, but produces the weird effect of turning the short A (as in *bad)* into an entirely different vowel, the short E (as in *bed)*.

Some Russians swing the short A in another direction, slapping the Union Jack on it and pronouncing it like a short O (as in *body*).

The key to producing an American short A is to lower the soft palate, keeping the sound out of the nose.

84

   ə   ə   ə   ə

ma<u>gic</u>, <u>per</u>so<u>nal</u>ity, stack, <u>al</u>bums, <u>laugh</u>ing, <u>ash</u>tray

I spent a lot of time *<u>trav</u>elling* in the *back* seat of that old <u>Bu</u>ick.

Can I *ask <u>Al</u>bert* something?

                                ə

The two of us *sat* there and <u>lis</u>tened.

                 ə

The *crash* <u>sound</u>ed like <u>some</u>thing *had* been knocked <u>o</u>ver.

            ə ə

Ca<u>ffeine</u> makes a <u>ter</u>rible <u>bed</u>time *snack*.

       ə   ə   ə

That <u>hasn</u>'t been my <u>great</u>est <u>prob</u>lem.

        ə   ə

I *have* a true <u>at</u>titude of <u>grat</u>itude.

          ə

That was an <u>ac</u>cident.

Jack is <u>tell</u>ing <u>Kath</u>erine not to look *back* or feel *sad* about things.

85

The 'OW' Sound

This vowel begins with a short A (as in *cat*), then picks up an *uh* sound. It appears in many words with *ou* spellings (such as *out*), and *ow* spellings (as in *down*). Because many Russians learn to speak English from British instructors, there is a tendency to begin this sound with a short O, which gives the vowel combination a rather old-fashioned, European flavor, so *cow* sounds like *cauw*. The American version leads with a short A.

now, without, crowd, south, <u>tow</u>er, howl, outside

86

        ə   ə   ə

She was <u>que</u>stioned *about* the en<u>coun</u>ter.

I'll look back at this a year from *now* and it will just be a blip on my <u>ra</u>dar.

   ə   ə

Suc<u>cess</u> comes *down* to <u>know</u>ing your <u>cus</u>tomers.

She was a such a clean freak that she must have come *out* of the womb with a can of <u>Ly</u>sol in one hand and a rag in the <u>oth</u>er.

I could still hear my <u>father</u> *shouting* *about* the *downstairs* <u>bed</u>room.

          ə   ə   ə

He re<u>turned</u> *hours* <u>la</u>ter and pre<u>tend</u>ed <u>noth</u>ing had <u>hap</u>pened.

                                     ə

I *found* myself <u>bit</u>ing back a gasp of re<u>lief</u>.

87

The *clouds* made a <u>thun</u>dering *sound*.

The *clown* <u>hur</u>ried *out* of the room.

Now look what you made us do.

I'll go see what this is *ab<u>out</u>*.

The plan was *sound*.

                                    ə   ə
Which part did you get the most en<u>joy</u>ment *out* of?

                            ə
My <u>mother</u> <u>understood</u> *how* to <u>han</u>dle my dad's <u>an</u>ger.

         ə
The <u>side</u>walks <u>gli</u>stened * on the *downtown* streets.

* glisten - to shine or sparkle

Use Common Words

This manual attempts to bring logic to the American accent—as much logic as one can bring to something involving a language thrown together for thousands of years and an accent that sprung from the collision of various cultures on a previously undiscovered continent.

Many Russians have expressed to me how overwhelming a task it seems to learn the designated syllable stress of every single English word. The very thought of such a monumental chore is enough to make one shudder. So may I suggest mastering a dozen or so words you use on a daily basis?

A number of frequently-used words should be employed to establish an American accent. By descending in pitch on the emphasized syllable, the speaker presents the rhythm required to communicate with Americans.

    ə   ə
<u>on</u>ly, what<u>ev</u>er, to<u>day</u>

                                          ə
There's <u>noth</u>ing <u>bet</u>ter than a <u>show</u>erhead that <u>chang</u>es <u>col</u>or based on <u>tem</u>perature.

              ə
It <u>al</u>most seemed <u>ter</u>rible that she would <u>nev</u>er know this hi<u>lar</u>ious fact.

      ə

I *didn't* know *anything* about it.

                        ə

She talks sports, and we all just *listen*.

Like *many* old <u>sold</u>iers, he wears white socks.

            ə   ə

I miss *being* a com<u>plete</u> <u>for</u>eigner and <u>hav</u>ing no ties to *anyone*.

Kids take your *money* and wreck your house.

                   ə ə   ə

From the *very* be<u>gin</u>ning, Los <u>An</u>geles was all about the <u>au</u>tomobile.

        ə

Unlike so *many people* around me, I know who I am.

The best words I *ever* said are the words that *never* left my mouth.

After a few days, I <u>fi</u>gured out what he *re<u>all</u>y* meant.

ə

You are *al<u>lowed</u>* to be *<u>happ</u>y*.

ə

I <u>under</u>stand <u>any</u>thing and <u>every</u>thing about <u>vod</u>ka.

ə

To<u>morr</u>ow is *a<u>noth</u>er* day.

ə

I *for<u>got</u>* to tell you something *im<u>port</u>ant*.

93

Taking Command

Americans tend to descend in pitch on stressed syllables, and they tend to stress certain verbs when giving instructions and offering suggestions.

The use of the imperative tense triggers the stressed syllable to descend in pitch.

call, go, watch, sleep

              ə   ə
Give up de<u>fi</u>ning yourself by what <u>happ</u>ened in the past.

ə   ə ə ə
A<u>void</u> <u>chan</u>ging from the o<u>ri</u>ginal plan.

                              ə
Pull up a stool in the <u>kitch</u>en.

     ə   ə   ə
Pick a pro<u>fess</u>ion that you think you'll en<u>joy</u>.

                    ə
Shut up and *leave* me a<u>lone</u>.

                     ə
Wrap up the <u>proj</u>ect to<u>day</u>.

Whisper in the <u>baby</u>'s ear.

                              ə   ə
Give them a fifteen-<u>min</u>ute <u>warn</u>ing to <u>fin</u>ish what<u>ev</u>er they are <u>do</u>ing.

Even when a request doesn't directly employ the imperative tense, the speaker of American English creates downward inflections on stressed syllables.

I *hope* that you're <u>set</u>tling in and have made some friends.

ə
I would *ad<u>vise</u>* you not to dis<u>close</u> your in<u>tense</u> <u>fee</u>lings.

Avoid Scratching the Initial H

Russian speakers tend to add a distracting, throaty sound to their *H*. It's not only Russians. Most of the world's languages use a scratch in the throat to help articulate a foreign relative of the letter H. When Americans pronounce an *H*, they do so with an open throat—one free of obstruction.

                              ə
home, <u>hu</u>ngry, high, <u>ho</u>bo, whole, <u>ha</u>ppening

            ə
The sun was *be<u>hind</u> him* now, the car <u>cha</u>sing its own <u>sha</u>dow.

      ə   ə
<u>Resurrec</u>tion is a <u>com</u>mon theme in *<u>hor</u>ror*.

           ə   ə

All <u>e</u>fforts to ex<u>tin</u>guish the fire *have* <u>en</u>d<u></u>ed in <u>fai</u>lure.

He loved *how his hands* felt when *he hit* the <u>base</u>ball.

To illustrate the difference, a Russian might butcher that last H-laden sentence:

Hhhe loved *hhauw hhhees hhendss* felt ven *hhhe heet* behhsball.

In this stereotypical example, the letter H scratches on numerous words, creating a sentence that an American would have a hard time understanding. The American H uses the least amount of breath necessary.

He loved *how his hands* felt when *he hit* the <u>base</u>ball.

       ə   ə
The en<u>tire</u> year *a<u>head</u>* was comp<u>lete</u>ly mapped out.

                               ə   ə
It *has* <u>on</u>ly been in the past *<u>hund</u>red* years that *<u>hum</u>an* beings *have* be<u>gun</u> to re<u>view</u> their *<u>child</u>hoods*.

It was good to *hear* that per<u>spec</u>tive.

Maintain *<u>healthy</u>* <u>bound</u>aries in *<u>hostile</u>* <u>plac</u>es.

We worked out the details as we <u>wandered</u> the dirt roads near my *home*, my <u>daugh</u>ter *<u>happily</u>* <u>walk</u>ing be<u>tween</u> us.

    ə
I <u>did</u>n't *have* to look *hard* to find them.

                                                ə
As soon as *<u>Henry</u>* knew *he had* the job, *he* be<u>gan</u> <u>brain</u>storming * <u>ideas</u>.

* brainstorming - the act of trying to think of ways to solve problems.

100

The Short O compared to the Short U

Russians have the tendency to confuse these two short vowels. This chapter reviews and compares the two sounds.

The short O appears in words such as *not, block* and *obvious*. Within this manual, the short O is represented by *ah*, as that is an approximation of how it sounds in spoken American English.

The short U appears in words such as *us, love* and <u>*some*</u>*times*. Americans pronounce it *uh*, so it is marked *uh* in this manual.

There are many words in English where the only difference is the vowel, so mastering these two short vowels is essential to being understood.

Read each column straight down, then left to right, comparing these two short vowels.

The Short U - uh	The Short O - ah
rub	rob
luck	lock
shut	shot
nut	not
duck	dock
buddy	body
gut	got
color	collar
wonder	wander
gun	gone
hut	hot

Read over the following sentences, determining if the words in italics are the short O (ah) or the short U (uh). Make a mark in pencil above each italicized word to indicate which sound the stressed syllable is, either *ah* (the short O) or *uh* (the short U).

UH/AH Drill

Do__nn__a tucked the *frog* into her blue jeans.

It was *Scott's* most *pro__vo__cative* work yet.

It's no *fun* *__stop__ping* if you'd *__rath__er* be *fl__y__ing*.

Tom could oc*__ca__sionally* be *__stub__born*.

I *__won__der* if *__Os__car* has *e__nough__* *__mon__ey* for the *bus*.

We re*__main__ed* six feet a*__part__* from *one* a*__noth__er*.

I cooked *__some__thing* for *__Rob__ert*.

UH/AH Drill - answers

   ah   uh   ah
Donna tucked the *frog* <u>in</u>to her blue jeans.

        ah   ah
It was *Scott's* most *pro<u>voc</u>ative* work yet.

     uh ah
It's no *fun <u>stop</u>ping* if you'd <u>rath</u>er be <u>fly</u>ing.

ah   uh
Tom could oc<u>cas</u>ionally be *<u>stub</u>born*.

 uh   ah   uh   uh   uh
I <u>won</u>der if *<u>Os</u>car* has *<u>enough</u> <u>mon</u>ey* for the *bus*.

                              uh uh
We re<u>mained</u> six feet a<u>part</u> from *one <u>an</u>other*.

     uh   ah
I cooked *<u>some</u>thing* for *<u>Rob</u>ert*.

Mastery Lesson #1

The following is a monologue from the stage play, "Hot Potato". In this passage, a hard drinker sings the praises of his favorite bar.

For the best use of this lesson, attempt to mark syllable stress. For example, in the sentence:

It's become an embarrassment of good fortune.

You'll need to underline the stressed syllable(s).

It's be<u>come</u> an em<u>bar</u>rassment of good <u>for</u>tune.

109

Speech #1

All things good and evil present themselves at the Hornet's Nest. We have pretty much all we need in this joint. A seemingly unlimited supply of beer and an assortment of good ole boys. Just eyeing the termite-infested welcome sign makes me feel all warm and squishy. This is it. A friendly watering hole where I can gingerly suck my vodka off the ice cubes. What Alexander Borodin did for music, I'm doing for the lost art of 'having a good time'. Hey, throw in a visit from the Sheriff, and it's become an embarrassment of good fortune. So I ask, is there such a thing as too much good karma? Hold on to your hat. This town is about to find out.

Speech #1 (syllable stress marked)

All things good and <u>ev</u>il pre<u>sent</u> themselves at the <u>Hor</u>net's Nest. We have <u>pret</u>ty much all we need in this joint. A <u>see</u>mingly un<u>lim</u>ited sup<u>ply</u> of beer and an as<u>sort</u>ment of good ole boys. Just <u>eye</u>ing the <u>ter</u>mite-in<u>fes</u>ted <u>wel</u>come sign makes me feel all warm and <u>squish</u>y. This is it. A <u>friend</u>ly <u>wat</u>ering hole where I can <u>gin</u>gerly suck my <u>vod</u>ka off the ice cubes. What <u>Al</u>exander <u>Bor</u>odin did for <u>mu</u>sic, I'm <u>do</u>ing for the lost art of '<u>hav</u>ing a good time'. Hey, throw in a <u>vis</u>it from the <u>Sher</u>iff, and it's be<u>come</u> an em<u>bar</u>rassment of good <u>for</u>tune. So I ask, is there such a thing as too much good <u>kar</u>ma? Hold on to your hat. This town is a<u>bout</u> to find out.

111

Foreigners are often asked if they can speak with an American accent. How can that be accomplished without a plan? Tools are needed—the most valuable being proper syllable stress.

Practice descending in pitch on stressed syllables:

p<u>re</u>tty, as<u>sort</u>ment, <u>seem</u>ingly un<u>lim</u>ited sup<u>ply</u>

All things good and *<u>ev</u>il pre<u>sent</u>* themselves at the *<u>Hor</u>net's* Nest.

Just *<u>ey</u>eing* the *<u>ter</u>mite-in<u>fes</u>ted <u>wel</u>come* sign makes me feel all warm and *<u>squish</u>y*.

Throw in a *<u>vis</u>it* from the *<u>Sher</u>iff*, and it's *be<u>come</u>* an *em<u>bar</u>rassment* of good *<u>for</u>tune*.

On the next page, mark where the unstressed vowel becomes a schwa, meaning that it reduces to 'uh', as opposed to being articulated as a full vowel. For example, the following sentence:

It's be<u>come</u> an em<u>bar</u>rassment of good <u>for</u>tune

... would be marked as:

       ə   ə   ə   ə
It's be<u>come</u> an em<u>bar</u>rassment of good <u>for</u>tune

Speech #1 (mark unstressed reduced vowels)

All things good and <u>e</u>vil pre<u>sent</u> themselves at the Hor<u>net</u>'s Nest. We have <u>pret</u>ty much all we need in this joint. A <u>seem</u>ingly un<u>lim</u>ited sup<u>ply</u> of beer and an as<u>sort</u>ment of good ole boys. Just <u>eye</u>ing the ter<u>mi</u>te-in<u>fes</u>ted <u>wel</u>come sign makes me feel all warm and <u>squish</u>y. This is it. A <u>friend</u>ly <u>wa</u>tering hole where I can <u>gin</u>gerly suck my <u>vod</u>ka off the ice cubes. What <u>Alex</u>an<u>der</u> <u>Bo</u>rodin did for <u>mu</u>sic, I'm <u>do</u>ing for the lost art of '<u>hav</u>ing a good time'. Hey, throw in a <u>vi</u>sit from the <u>Sher</u>iff, and it's be<u>come</u> an em<u>bar</u>rassment of good <u>for</u>tune. So I ask, is there such a thing as too much good <u>kar</u>ma? Hold on to your hat. This town is a<u>bout</u> to find out.

Speech #1 (syllable stress and ə inserted)

                     ə   ə

All things good and <u>ev</u>il pre<u>sent</u> themselves at the

  ə

<u>Hor</u>net's Nest. We have <u>pret</u>ty much all we need in

                  ə   ə   ə

this joint. A <u>see</u>mingly un<u>lim</u>ited sup<u>ply</u> of beer and

   ə   ə

an as<u>sort</u>ment of good ole boys. Just <u>eye</u>ing the

        ə   ə

<u>ter</u>mite-in<u>fes</u>ted <u>wel</u>come sign makes me feel all

warm and <u>squish</u>y. This is it. A <u>friend</u>ly <u>wat</u>ering

                             ə

hole where I can <u>gin</u>gerly suck my <u>vod</u>ka off the ice

         ə   ə ə

cubes. What <u>Al</u>exander <u>Bo</u>rodin did for <u>mu</u>sic, I'm

<u>do</u>ing for the lost art of '<u>hav</u>ing a good time'. Hey,

throw in a v*i*sit from the Sh*e*riff, and it's bec*o*me an

emb*a*rrassment of good f*o*rtune. So I ask, is there

such a thing as too much good k*a*rma? Hold on to

your hat. This town is ab*ou*t to find out.

Be sure that unstressed syllables remain unstressed. This is best achieved by descending in pitch on stressed syllables. Americans don't make a conscious decision to reduce certain unstressed vowels. That reduction grows out of their tendency to fall in pitch on stressed syllables.

    ə   ə   ə   ə
evil, welcome, karma, Hornet's Nest

             ə   ə   ə
Throw in a visit from the Sheriff, and it's become an

   ə   ə   ə
embarrassment of good fortune.

A friendly watering hole where I can gingerly suck

   ə
my vodka off the ice cubes.

Take advantage of the times when the letter S becomes a final Z. Be sure to eliminate as much air as possible when voicing a Z, opting to have the sound resonate in your jaw, throat and chest.

Note: In the upcoming final drill of this lesson, a **Z** will be drawn above the sound to remind you articulate this voiced consonant.

    Z   Z Z   Z Z

things, themselves, boys, ice cubes, is

        Z   Z

All *things* good and <u>ev</u>il pre<u>sent</u> *themselves* at the <u>Hornet</u>'s Nest.

A <u>seem</u>ingly un<u>lim</u>ited sup<u>ply</u> of beer and an
$$Z$$
as<u>sort</u>ment of good ole *boys*.

Consider how distracting a mispronounced, breathy Z

is to the American ear.

Note: the following examples are *incorrect*.
       S
ice cubes
       S
This is it.

Endeavor to eliminate squeakiness when voicing a Z.

This is best accomplished by first stopping the sound

in the throat, then allowing tone to vibrate, creating a

Z.

A <u>frien</u>dly <u>wa</u>tering hole where I can <u>gin</u>gerly suck
$$Z$$
my <u>vod</u>ka off the ice *cubes*.

    Z

This *is* it.

The short A (as in *bad*) needs to remain flat, neither becoming a short E (as in *bed*) or becoming a short O (as in *body*). Because of the variety of ways the Russian speaker may mispronounce the short A, it is important to keep tabs on the vowel. Become aware of common spelling cues for the short A, most frequently the letter A before a single consonant (as in *hat*) or a consonant cluster (as in *ask*).

Note: In the upcoming summary of this lesson, the short A will be represented by the commonly accepted symbol æ which will be marked above the sound to remind you to create a short A.

121

 æ æ   æ æ
have, <u>Alex</u>ander, ask, hat

   æ

We *have* <u>pret</u>ty much all we need in this joint.

   æ

What <u>Alex</u>ander <u>Bor</u>odin did for <u>mus</u>ic, I'm <u>do</u>ing for

      æ

the lost art of '<u>*hav*</u>*ing* a good time'.

   æ

So I *ask*, is there such a thing as too much good <u>kar</u>ma?

        æ

Hold on to your hat.

Now it's time to put it all together. Follow the notations to descend in pitch on stressed syllables, reduce certain unstressed vowels, articulate the final Z on select endings, and produce the American short A.

123

Speech #1 (Final drill)

      Z   ə   ə   Z
All things good and and <u>evi</u>l pre<u>sent</u> themselves at the

  ə   æ
<u>Hor</u>net's Nest. We have <u>pret</u>ty much all we need in

           ə   ə   ə
this joint. A <u>see</u>mingly un<u>lim</u>ited sup<u>ply</u> of beer and

   ə   ə   Z
an as<u>sort</u>ment of good ole boys. Just <u>eye</u>ing the

      ə   ə
<u>ter</u>mite-in<u>fes</u>ted <u>wel</u>come sign makes me feel all

             Z
warm and <u>squ</u>ishy. This is it. A <u>friend</u>ly <u>wat</u>ering

                ə
hole where I can <u>gin</u>gerly suck my <u>vod</u>ka off the ice

Z   ə   əə
cubes. What <u>Alex</u>ander <u>Bo</u>rodin did for <u>mu</u>sic, I'm

            æ
<u>do</u>ing for the lost art of '<u>hav</u>ing a good time'. Hey,

              ə   ə   ə
throw in a v<u>i</u>sit from the <u>Sh</u>eriff, and it's be<u>come</u> an

     ə   ə   ə   æ
emb<u>a</u>rrassment of good <u>fo</u>rtune. So I ask, is there

                   z   ə
such a thing as too much good <u>ka</u>rma? Hold on to

       æ   ə
your hat. This town is a<u>bout</u> to find out.

Mastery Lesson #2

The following is taken from the suspense novel "Violent Delights". In this passage, a man brings his lover to a riverbank that holds special significance in his life.

Read over the text, taking time to mark the syllable stress.

Speech #2

I thought I would share one of my favorite places with you. They named it Scavenger Point. It was built as a publicity stunt one Halloween. The city thought it might become a place to celebrate seasonal holidays. Oktoberfests. Easter-egg hunts. If memory serves, it wasn't always halfway underwater. The river rose. They're still doing construction. American thinking. If a bad idea doesn't pan out, it must mean you need to sink twice as much money into it. They're trying to install a pier, but there's no foundation, so the pier keeps sinking. I used to come here as a boy, before the city dreamed of making it an attraction. If you ignore the farce that man is playing out with the construction, you're treated to a canvass painted by the hand of God. Now, I don't believe in religion, but looking at all this, I allow for the scientific possibility.

128

Speech #2 (syllable stress marked)

I thought I would share one of my fa<u>vo</u>rite <u>pla</u>ces with you. They named it <u>Sca</u>venger Point. It was built as a pu<u>bli</u>city stunt one <u>Hal</u>loween. The <u>ci</u>ty thought it might be<u>come</u> a place to <u>ce</u>lebrate <u>sea</u>sonal <u>ho</u>lidays. Ok<u>to</u>berfests. <u>Eas</u>ter-egg hunts. If <u>me</u>mory serves, it <u>was</u>n't <u>al</u>ways <u>half</u>way <u>un</u>der<u>wa</u>ter. The <u>ri</u>ver rose. They're still <u>do</u>ing con<u>struc</u>tion. A<u>me</u>rican <u>thin</u>king. If a bad i<u>dea</u> <u>does</u>n't pan out, it must mean you need to sink twice as much <u>mo</u>ney <u>in</u>to it. They're <u>try</u>ing to in<u>stall</u> a pier, but there's no foun<u>da</u>tion, so the pier keeps <u>sin</u>king. I used to come here as a boy, be<u>fore</u> the <u>ci</u>ty dreamed of <u>ma</u>king it an at<u>trac</u>tion. If you i<u>gnore</u> the farce that man is <u>play</u>ing out with the con<u>struc</u>tion, you're treated to a canvass painted by the hand of God. Now, I don't believe in religion, but looking at all this, I allow for the scientific possibility.

130

Make the most of the American stress pattern by descending in pitch when pronouncing words with designated syllable stress.

ə   ə   ə   ə   ə ə
favorite places, scavenger, American thinking

ə   ə ə
I don't be<u>lieve</u> in re<u>li</u>gion, but <u>look</u>ing at all this, I al<u>low</u> for the <u>scien</u>tific pos<u>si</u>bility.

It was built as a pu<u>bli</u>city stunt one <u>Hal</u>loween.

                       ə   ə
The <u>ci</u>ty thought it might be<u>come</u> a place to <u>cele</u>brate <u>sea</u>sonal <u>ho</u>lidays.

                            ə
If <u>memo</u>ry serves, it <u>wasn't</u> <u>al</u>ways <u>half</u>way <u>under</u>water.

They're <u>try</u>ing to in<u>stall</u> a pier, but there's no foun<u>da</u>tion, so the pier keeps <u>sink</u>ing.

Use the long A (as in *save, way,* and *faint*) to both establish a clear vowel and to descend in pitch. A Russian speaker should make sure the long A does not become the short E (as in *set* or *went*).

In this series of drills, and later in the final walkthrough of the lesson, the long A will be represented by this symbol Ā

   Ā   Ā   Ā   Ā   Ā
named, *pla*y*ing*, *painted*, *ce*l*ebrate*, *ma*k*ing*

                                      Ā   Ā
I thought I would share one of my *fa*v*orite* *pla*c*es* with you.

            Ā
There's no *foun*d*ation*, so the pier keeps *sin*k*ing*.

       Ā   Ā
It *wa*s*n't* *a*l*ways* *hal*f*way* *un*d*er*w*ater*.

Be sure to pronounce the Long O (as in *go* and *sold*) as an American. For the speaker of Russian, that means avoiding two possible pitfalls.

The first priority is to avoid a British tone, which would be mispronounced 'eah-O'.

The Russian speaker must also avoid reducing the long O into something resembling the AW sound (as in *jaw* and *talk*).

In this section, and at the end of this mastery lesson, the long O will be marked **Ō**

Ō   Ō
rose, Okt<u>ober</u>fests

         Ō   Ō
There's *no* foun<u>dat</u>ion, *so* the pier keeps <u>sink</u>ing.

   Ō
I *don't* be<u>lieve</u> in re<u>lig</u>ion.

Pronounce the Long E (as in *he* and *really*) as an American, both when it appears in stressed syllables (as in *agreed*) and when it appears in unstressed syllables (as in *wonderfully*).

In this lesson, and during its final recap, the long E is marked Ē

    Ē   Ē Ē   Ē Ē   Ē
pu<u>bli</u>city, <u>ci</u>ty, <u>Eas</u>ter, <u>me</u>mory, <u>sea</u>sonal, dreamed, <u>trea</u>ted, pos<u>si</u>bility

      Ē   Ē   Ē
It must *mean* you *need* to sink twice as much *<u>mo</u>ney* <u>in</u>to it.

     Ē
I don't *be<u>lie</u>ve* in re<u>li</u>gion.

During this final runthrough, address all the issues that were covered. Work toward mastering this handful of concepts, including syllable stress, as well as the long A, the long O, and the long E.

136

Speech #2 (final drill)

                                            Ā   Ā ə

I thought I would share one of my fa<u>vo</u>rite <u>pla</u>ces with

            Ā   ə

you. They named it <u>Sca</u>venger Point. It was built as a

ə   Ē   ə Ē   Ē

pu<u>bli</u>city stunt one <u>Hall</u>oween. The <u>city</u> thought it

    ə   Ā   əĀ Ēəə   Ā

might be<u>come</u> a place to <u>ce</u>lebrate <u>sea</u>sonal <u>ho</u>lidays.

  Ō   Ē   Ē

Ok<u>to</u>berfests. <u>Eas</u>ter-egg hunts. If <u>mem</u>ory serves, it

ə   Ā   Ā   Ō

<u>was</u>n't <u>al</u>ways <u>half</u>way <u>un</u>de<u>rwa</u>ter. The <u>ri</u>ver rose.

           ə   ə ə   əə

They're still <u>do</u>ing con<u>struc</u>tion. A<u>mer</u>ican <u>think</u>ing. If

137

       ə   Ē   Ē
a bad <u>idea</u> <u>does</u>n't pan out, it must mean you need to

                      Ē
sink twice as much <u>mo</u>ney <u>in</u>to it. They're <u>try</u>ing to

                            Ō   Ā ə   Ō
in<u>stall</u> a pier, but there's no foun<u>da</u>tion, so the pier

Ē   ə
keeps <u>sink</u>ing. I used to come here as a boy, be<u>fore</u>

   Ē Ē   Ā   ə   ə
the <u>ci</u>ty dreamed of <u>ma</u>king it an at<u>trac</u>tion. If you

                                Ā
ig<u>nore</u> the farce that man is <u>play</u>ing out with the

ə   ə   Ē ə   ə Ā ə
con<u>struc</u>tion, you're <u>treat</u>ed to a <u>can</u>vass <u>paint</u>ed by

138

                        Ō   ə   Ē   ə   ə
the hand of God. Now, I don't be<u>lie</u>ve in re<u>lig</u>ion, but

                            ə   ə   ə
<u>look</u>ing at all this, I al<u>low</u> for the <u>sci</u>en<u>tif</u>ic

   ə   ə Ē
pos<u>si</u>bi<u>li</u>ty.

Final Notes

A common complaint echoed throughout my classes is that adults wish they had started studying accent reduction much sooner. Their words are laced with deep regret. I assure them that the adult mind is far better suited to learn the American accent than a child's, who only seem to improve on a miraculously-rapid basis because it has all day to concern itself with nothing but education. In my experience, children are like hand grenades; their patience has a time limit and then they explode. The adult can generally grasp something in one hour that the child might struggle with for an indefinite length of time.

Consider reviewing this manual on a regular basis. Studying can be a terrific—and safe—stress reducer, with no risk of a torn ligament or a hangover.

Accent reduction may be the universal headscratcher. I'd be lying if I said it is all roses and candy canes. But as the saying goes, "He who dares, wins." Those determined few who address their speech are generally cut from tougher stock. They are strongly motivated, and embrace the challenge of applying these guidelines to their everyday speech. The results are flourishing improvement and better communication.

Acknowledgments

Allow me first to thank **Pete Sain** for the cover (his eighth for my projects!) Anyone admiring the range of his styles (from horror to sci-fi to anime to education) is sure to appreciate his talent.

Most students wander into my classroom with a sad look on their face. Not **Claudia Zielke**, who embraced my suggestions and now displays mastery of the subject.

Alimorad Farshchian's passion for mastering American English inspired this manual.

Thank you to all my students, including **Irina Kelly**. Their willingness helped me pat out the wrinkle of my method, and continue to fill me with gratitude.

About the Author

Despite my Russian name, I was born and raised in New York City—and once had the accent to prove it. As a young actor living in Manhattan, my speech was so impenetrable that it had a presence of its own. I lost out on opportunities because of it. Unwilling to take those experiences with me into my career, I vowed an end had come to the rookie mistakes.

I studied with coaches, read books on the subject, and sought to develop a standard American accent that possessed a texture so real, no artifice could be heard.

When I moved to Los Angeles, I left my accent in a closet on Lexington Avenue. I believe a tourist traded for it at a pawn shop for a Russian hat. That's not true. What actually happened was a drunk was tricked into accepting my old New York accent after he lost a bet with a retired tour guide. Wherever my accent wound up, it didn't make the trip west. There was no room for it on my checklist.

I began teaching accents in California in 1996 within the Community Services departments of Los Angeles' City and Valley Colleges. After years of teaching speech-related classes, I'm thrilled to present you with the tools to attain mastery of your accent.

I continue to teach privately, both from my studio in Hollywood and via Skype worldwide.

Ivan Borodin

1626 N. Wilcox Avenue #490

Los Angeles, California 90028

IvanPresents@gmail.com

office (323) 319-4826

Skype handle: IvanBorodinUSA

The following books would also serve you quite well in developing clear American speech.

Accent Reduction: The Standard American Accent
by Ivan Borodin

If speaking American English is a recurring problem, this concise manual will help you be understood in the conversation circle. The hard work has already been done for you, as this guide features the vowels needed to sound American in no time.

Accent Reduction: Using Consonants to Sound American
by Ivan Borodin

Trying to speak with an American accent shouldn't leave one feeling like they've lost large amounts of their self-esteem. Having taught accent reduction for two decades, this instructor felt compelled to share a unique approach to mastery—using the humble consonants. Follow the drills in this extensive manual, and speaking engagements will become less like a crime scene, and more like a realized opportunity.

Both courses are supported by YouTube videos

Also by Ivan Borodin

Accent Reduction
Accent Reduction for Spanish Speakers
Accent Annihilation for Japanese Speakers
Eliminate Your Korean Accent
Lose Your German Accent

Dialect Training
Learn a Southern Drawl
Learn a Wicked Awesome Boston Accent
Speak with a New York Accent
Speak with an Accent

Fiction
The Martian Shuffle
Pandora 2011: Accounts of the Cursed Shopping Center
Pandora 2012: Southern Belles
Pandora 2013: Hullabaloo
Violent Delights

Stage Plays
Hot Potato
Play Rough

Made in United States
Orlando, FL
27 May 2024